The Little Entomologist

Mere Mortals

The Little Entomologist

A poem
by
Roxanne Hoffman

with illustrations
by
Edward Odwitt

POETS WEAR PRADA • Hoboken, New Jersey

The Little Entomologist

First North American Publication 2018

Copyright © 2018 Roxanne Hoffman & Edward Odwitt

All rights reserved. Except for use in any review or for educational purposes, the reproduction or utilization of this work in whole or in part in any form by electronic, mechanical or other means, now known or hereafter invented, including xerography, photocopying and recording, or in any informational or retrieval system, is forbidden without the written permission of the publisher.

Poets Wear Prada
533 Bloomfield Street
Second Floor
Hoboken, NJ 07030
http://pwpbooks.blogspot.com/

Grateful acknowledgment is made to Sam Dot Publishing and editor Cathy Buburuz who first published this poem in *Champagne Shivers*. And to Susan Maurer who urged the poet to send out her work and recommended that publication as a possible home for the poem. Special thanks to Jack Cooper for his astute editorial suggestions and meticulous attention to detail in the final preparation of this volume.

ISBN: 978-1-946116-03-1

Printed in the U.S.A.

Poetry: Roxanne Hoffman
Front cover and interior illustrations: Edward Odwitt

In Fond Memory of
Brant Lyon
&
For Diane Faith

contents

They said she stripped the mighty Monarchs / 3
And would not crunch them underfoot / 4
Served up as opportune hors d'oeuvres / 7
Squads of chirping sparrows, mousy brown / 8
Meanwhile, she kept her precious prize / 11
Treasured trophies to be later marveled / 12

~ *illustrations* ~

Mere Mortals / faceplate
Their Black-Edged Fiery Wings / (facing page 3)
Crunch Them Underfoot / 5
Opportune Hors d'Oeuvres / 6
Hopeful at the Sight / 9
Her Precious Prize / 10
Treasured Trophies / 13

about the author / 14
about the artist / 15

The Little Entomologist

Their Black-Edged Fiery Wings

The Little Entomologist

They said she stripped the mighty Monarchs
of their black-edged fiery wings,
reduced these majestic creatures to mere mortals,
returned to kiss the earth — flightless fledglings,

And would not crunch them underfoot
to still their pulsing frames to final rest
but left them wriggling like baited
worms as she continued on her quest,

Crunch Them Underfoot

Opportune Hors d'Oeuvres

Served up as opportune hors d'oeuvres,
to be gobbled up by scores of hungry birds
swooping down from trees and rooftop nests —
screeching starlings, spiny backed, glistening with
 iridescent jet;

Squads of chirping sparrows, mousy brown, perched
   on spindle legs
(cousins to the well-regarded goldfinch but
   considered birddom's dregs) —
hopping, hopeful, at the sight of so delectable a
   display,
scrambling to feast upon the spoils of our Little
   Entomologist's foray.

Hopeful at the Sight

Her Precious Prize

Meanwhile, she kept her precious prize tucked
   beneath her chin,
making her way back home, steadily, in slow motion,
caged within the hollow between cupped palms,
   hands embraced,
veering to avoid the curious and those in haste —

Treasured trophies to be later marveled under lens,
before mounted under glass to join the woven nest
   of wrens,
high upon the shelf for prominent display
alongside marble keepsies and the lapis-blue feather
   of the jay.

Treasured Trophies

about the author

Roxanne Hoffman left her old haunts on Wall Street to answer a patient hotline for a New York home healthcare provider, and observes that most folks would rather be dead than broke. A member of the Vampire Empire, the Bram Stoker Memorial Association and the International Society for the Study of Ghosts and Apparitions, she's always had a yen for Death and the unnatural.

Her poems and stories have been sighted, on and off the net, appearing and reappearing in literary journals — *Champagne Shivers, Danse Macabre, Dark Eye Glances, Dark Gothic Resurrected Magazine, Hospital Drive, House of Horror, Lucid Rhythms, Mirror Dance, The Pedestal Magazine, Scarlet Literary Magazine,* and *SNM Horror Magazine* — and can be heard during the 2005 indie flick, *Love & The Vampire,* directed by Dave Gold. Her take on divorce, "Macabre! Macabre!" was selected for inclusion in *House of Horror Best of 2009 Anthology*. The lyrics to "Rattle Them Bones," a song celebrating ghostdom, were selected for *House of Horror Best of 2010 Anthology* and nominated for a Pushcart Prize.

about the artist

Independent author and artist Edward Odwitt (aka Shawn Christopher Martin) is an enigma. His portfolio varies from symmetrical illustrations to graphics and pastels, and includes cartoons drawn primarily in black pen or pencil.

He is the author of *Head for the Hills* and *House of Haunts and Horrors*, illustrated books written for middleschool audiences. A limited-edition compilation of his artwork was published in 2013.

About The Type

Text is set in Andalus, a TrueType font (designed for both the screen display and printing) originally developed in 1993 by Glyph Systems, Limited Partnership, based in Andover, MA. It was later adapted in 2011 by Monotype.

Andalus is characterized by compressed character spacing, generous line spacing, sloping shoulders (h, m, n), above average x-heights (taller lowercase letters), lining numerals (figures are the same height as capital letters), non-lining (lowercase) colons, bracketed serifs (curves connect the serif to the stroke) which are angled on the heads of lowercase letters, a ridiculously exaggerated loop descending from the lowercase g, and the memorable flourish of swash on the tail of the capital Q.

This Arabic font, one of sixteen offered as a set by Glyph Systems., is named after Al-Andalus, or Islamic Iberia, a medieval Muslim territory that included Spain, Portugal, and part of southern France from 711 to 1492.

Traditionally, Microsoft made Andalus readily available to its customers as part of its Window and Office offerings, but with Windows 10 the font was moved into optional features, as the font was primarily intended for Arabic script, not for English.

We've selected it here for its Goth look. Above average x-height recalls classic children's books. The long lines of the poem are well served by Andalus's compressed character spacing while its generous line spacing make them easier to read, though admittedly the punctuation often seems to be absorbed.

www.ingramcontent.com/pod-product-compliance
Lightning Source LLC
Chambersburg PA
CBHW071805040426
42446CB00012B/2717